To Bodhi,

Enjoy!

Andrew [illegible]

hi·stories®

ALLIGATOR GRAHAM BELL

Based on the life of the great inventor, Alexander Graham Bell

Written and Illustrated by:
ANDREW TOFFOLI

ALLIGATOR GRAHAM BELL

Printed in China

ISBN 978-0-9763233-8-9

Library of Congress Control Number: 2011901292

Our mission is to educate children about history while using humor and imagination to teach valuable life lessons.

Please visit us online at: **www.littlegerm.com**

10 9 8 7 6 5 4 3 2 1

For Teddy

Alligator Graham Bell,
n ingenious reptile, was born in
Edinburgh, Scotland in 1847.

As a young alligator,
Al was always fascinated
by how people produced sound.

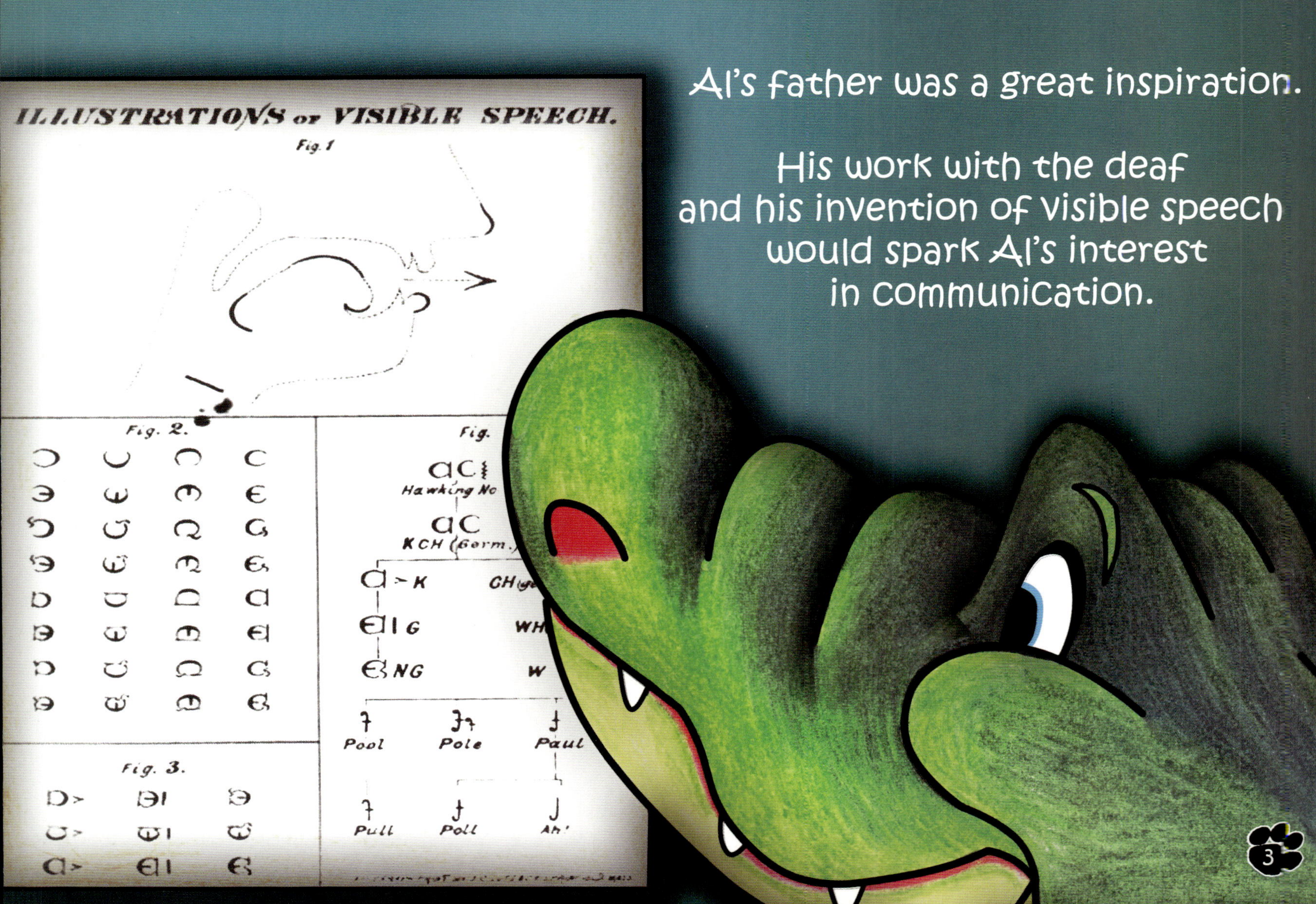

Al's father was a great inspiration.

His work with the deaf
and his invention of visible speech
would spark Al's interest
in communication.

Al exclaimed,
" When I grow up
I want to be just like my pop.
I will teach and invent
until I reach the top!"

Al became a teacher for the deaf
and worked on experiments
in the summertime.

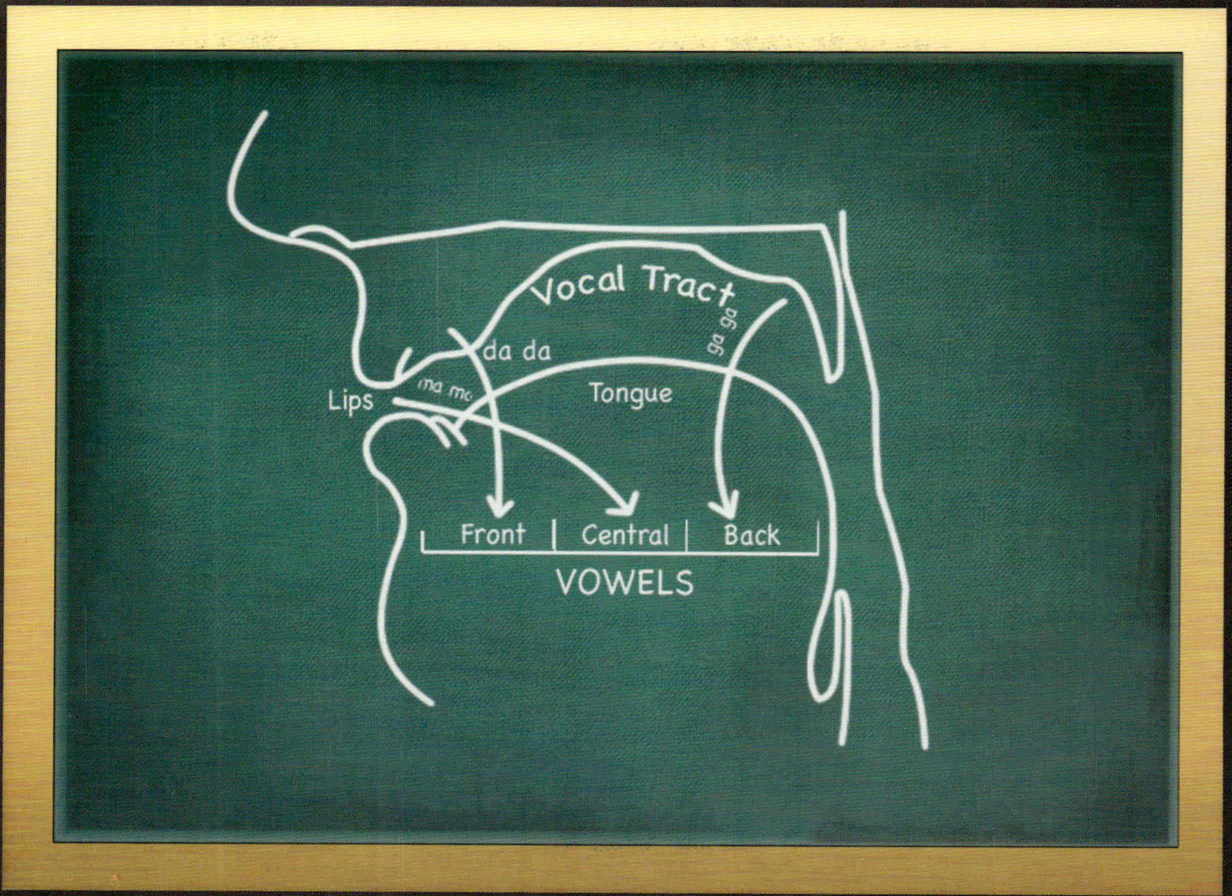

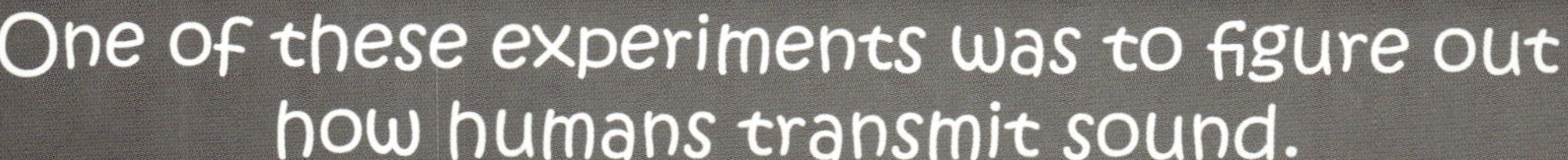

One of these experiments was to figure out how humans transmit sound.

Al began to read
and the work of Von Helmholtz
planted a seed.

After reading,
Al wanted to experiment with
words being transmitted by a wire.

For help,
Thomas Watson was hired.

Al and Tom were fascinated by the telegraph.
It was a machine that sent sounds by a wire
to places all over the world.

Hello

But Al and Tom were not content with just sounds...
to send words would be profound!

DO NOT DISTURB!

LIFE CHANGING INVENTION IN PROGRESS!

So, Al and Thomas began to work on a machine that sent the sound of a person's voice over a wire.

So they worked...

and worked...

and worked...

Until... they assembled
a prototype for the telephone.

It was time for the big test.

Al spoke these words into the telephone:
“Mr. Watson, come here.
I want to see you.”

And in the other room,
with his ear pressed
next to the receiver...

Thomas could not believe his ear!

He heard every word
and it made them cheer!

The celebration would have to be postponed,
as they rushed to Washington D.C.
to get the patent for the telephone.

Others had been working on the
same invention you see,

but Al and Tom made it first...
luckily!

The United States government
gave Al and Tom the patent.
The patent gave them the
exclusive right to make, use
and sell the telephone.

Next, Al and Tom went to Philadelphia for the World's Fair and they showed the telephone to all who were there.

Scientists and inventors from all over the world
could not believe their eyes
and gave the telephone
the grand prize.

Before Al put the
telephone in the mail,
he improved it
and then put it for sale

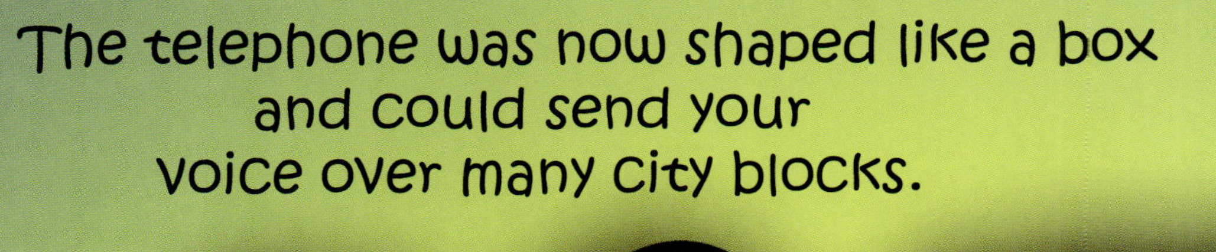

The telephone was now shaped like a box
and could send your
voice over many city blocks.

People stood in lines for days.
The Bell Telephone Company could not keep up with the craze.

Even though your loved ones lived far away, with the telephone, you could talk to them anytime of the day.

By 1900,
Al had installed 800,000
telephones in the United States.

Alligator Graham Bell's
curiosity, perseverance, patience
and problem solving led
to the creation of the most
revolutionary invention
of all time:

The telephone.

Words to know:

Curiosity: Noun-the desire to learn or know.

Inspiration: Noun- an action, thought, person, or other influence that inspires.

Profound: Adjective- having a deep and thorough understanding.

Prototype: Noun- an original model.

Reptile: Noun- an animal that crawls or moves on its belly or on small short legs.

Telephone: Noun- a system used to send speech or data over distances using a device calle a telephone that functions as the transmitter and receiver.

Transmit: Verb- to send from one person or place to another.

Coming Soon
from
hi·stories®
George
Washington
Carfur™
Ludpig Van
Beethoven™
Abrahound
Lincoln™
Marco Hippolo™

JoHorn Gutenberg™

Juan Ponce De LeBison™

Bark Twain™

Sir Ibis Newton™

Namolean Bonaparte™